More & More

Microwave

S'mores

Written by Tami Parker

When winter winds blow, everyone wants a tasty treat to tickle their toes and warm their nose.

What could possibly be better than some ooey, gooey s'mores to share with your friends?

Don't have a campfire, but still want the delicious taste of melted chocolate mixed with creamy marshmallows?

If your answer is YES, then no need to fear as long as a microwave is near. Come on. Let me show you how.

INGREDIENTS:

1 whole graham cracker
½ of a chocolate bar
1 large marshmallow

½ of a chocolate bar

1 large marshmallow

1 whole graham cracker

Makes one serving

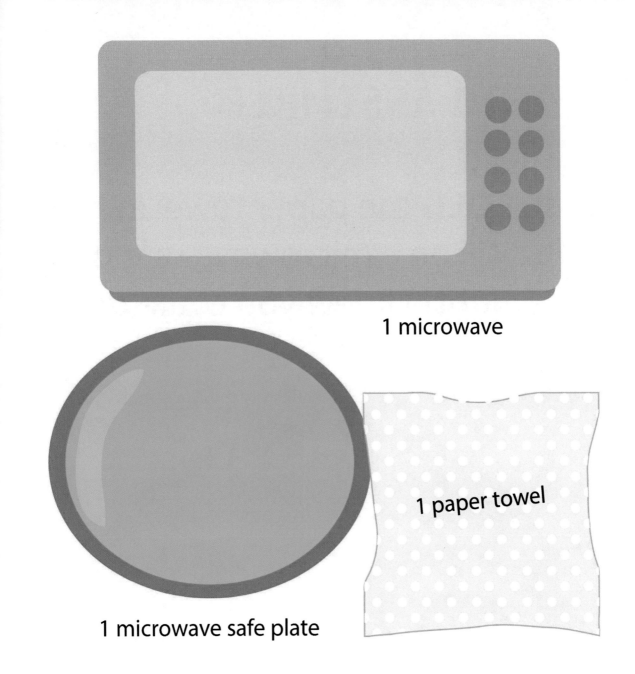

1 microwave

1 microwave safe plate

1 paper towel

MATERIALS NEEDED:

1 paper towel
1 microwave safe plate
1 microwave

6

READY TO ASSEMBLE:

First, **FOLD** the paper towel in half and **PLACE** on a microwave safe plate. Simple, right? I knew you could do it.

Second, **SNAP** the graham cracker in half. Be careful to **DIVIDE** the graham cracker into 2 perfect sections.

However, if it doesn't perfectly divide, don't worry. I have a solution.

If one of the sections is bigger than the other, **USE** the larger one for this step. See, easy solution.

Third, **PLACE** one of the graham cracker sections on the folded paper towel.

Without sneaking a bite, **PLACE** the chocolate bar on top of your graham cracker.

You didn't nibble, did you? That must have been hard. GREAT JOB!

Next, **SET** the marshmallow on top of the chocolate bar.

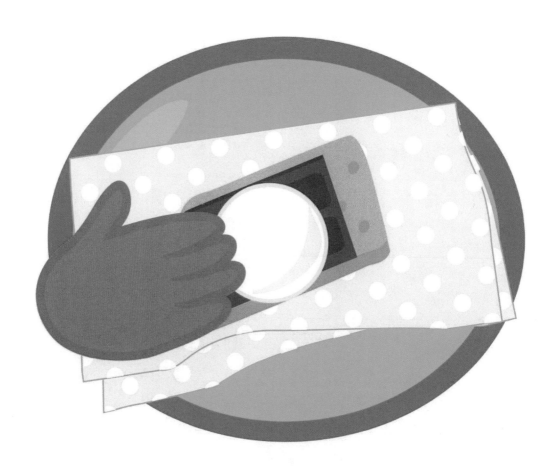

It won't be long before you taste that ooey, gooey goodness.

Carefully **POSITION** the last graham cracker on the very top.

This is where those building skills will be utilized. Be careful not to let that graham cracker fall!

Carefully **PICK** the microwave safe plate up and gently **PLACE** in the microwave.

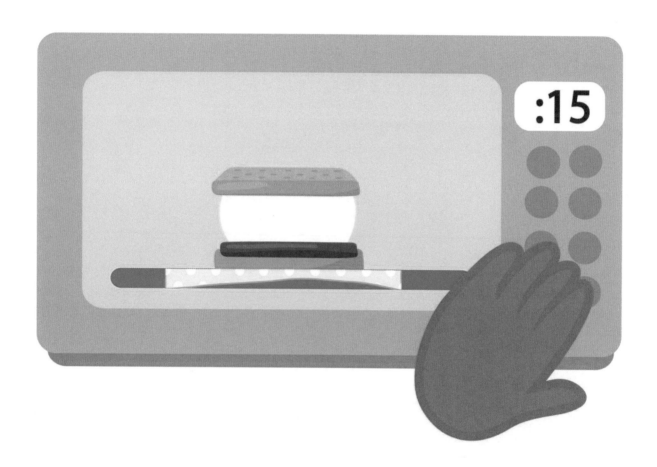

With an adult's help, **HEAT** on high for **15 seconds**.

Let **COOL** just a bit. Then, **TAKE** a bite of the ooey, gooey deliciousness. Even better, **SHARE** with a friend.

VARiETY:

There are so many different ways to add variety to your s'mores.

Instead of using plain marshmallows, try gingerbread, chocolate, cinnamon bun, strawberry, or french vanilla.

Another idea is to trade your chocolate bar for one of the many other varieties available.

For example, try cookies and cream, creamy caramel, or mint chocolate instead.

Want even more variety? Switch your honey flavored graham crackers for vanilla, cinnamon, or even chocolate flavored ones.

See, that's it. It was so simple, and you didn't need that campfire after all.

More & More

S'mores

Now, if you ever want MORE, you know "how to" make MORE and MORE S'MORES.

GLOSSARY:

Chocolate - a food made from roasted cacao beans

Gooey - soft and sticky

Graham - whole wheat flour that has not been sifted

Marshmallow- a soft, spongy treat made from sugar and gelatin

Microwave- kitchen appliance that cooks food with electromagnetic waves

Position- the way something is arranged or placed

DEDICATION PAGE

Dedicated to my AWESOME daughter, Billie-Jean, who always believed in me, even when I didn't believe myself.

ABOUT THE AUTHOR:

Tami Parker is a children's librarian and former classroom teacher. When she isn't surrounded by shelves and shelves of books, as well as children, she can be found in her home office creating even more books. For more information, visit her blog at obsessedwithlearning.com and her Teachers Pay Teachers store, Obsessed with Learning. Oh, you might also catch her eating some s'mores, as well.

Made in the USA
Columbia, SC
12 May 2021